Charming Guest Rooms

Be not Forgetful to entertain Strangers ~ for Thereby Some have entertained Angels unawares.

Hebrews 13:2

Charming Guest Rooms

Decorating Secrets from Country Inns

Mickey Baskett

&

Phyllis Mueller

Sterling Publishing Co., Inc.

New York

Prolific Impressions Production Staff

Editor in Chief: Mickey Baskett
Creative Director: Susan E. Mickey
Copy Editor: Phyllis Mueller
Graphics: Dianne Miller, Karen Turpin
Styling: Kirsten Jones
Photography: Jerry Mucklow, David Bjurstrom
Administration: Jim Baskett

Library of Congress Cataloging-in-Publication Data Available

10 9 8 7 6 5 4 3 2 1

Published in paperback in 2005 by Sterling Publishing Co., Inc.
387 Park Avenue South, New York, N.Y. 10016
© 2003 by Prolific Impressions, Inc.

Produced by Prolific Impressions, Inc.
160 South Candler St., Decatur, GA 30030

Distributed in Canada by Sterling Publishing,
% Canadian Manda Group, 165 Dufferin Street,
Toronto, Ontario, Canada M6K 3H6
Distributed in Great Britain and Europe by Chrysalis Books Group PLC,
The Chrysalis Building, Bramley Road, London W10 6SP, England
Distributed in Australia by Capricorn Link (Australia) Pty. Ltd.
P.O. Box 704, Windsor, NSW 2756 Australia

Printed in China
All rights reserved

Sterling ISBN 0-8069-6883-4 Hardcover
         ISBN 1-4027-2801-8 Paperback

For information about custom editions, special sales, premium and corporate purchases, please contact Sterling Special Sales Department at 800-805-5489 or specialsales@sterlingpub.com.

Acknowledgements

Thanks to the many people who allowed us into their homes to photograph their guest rooms. Special thanks for their unique contributions to:

Barrie and Bobby Aycock of the Glen-Ella Springs Inn, 1789 Bear Gap Road, Clarkesville, Georgia 30523. For reservations or information, visit www.glenella.com, email info@glen-ella.com, or call 706-754-7295.

De and Mike Kennedy of the Five Gables Inn, P.O. Box 335, 107 Murray Hill Road, East Boothbay, Maine 04544. For reservations or information, visit www.fivegablesinn.com, email info@fivegablesinn.com, or call 800-451-5048.

Lorrie Cook from Pierce & Parker in St. Simons, Georgia for allowing us to photograph homes she has decorated.

Plaid Enterprises, Inc. (www.plaid online.com) for supplying FolkArt® brand acrylic paints, Stencil Décor® stencils, and Royal Coat® decoupage finish for projects in this book.

Bill Thomsen and Thomsen Ltd. (www.thomsenltd.com) for allowing us to photograph their custom-made furniture.

Old Edna says, "Well...La de Da?", Hwy 227 and Price Canyon Rd., San Luis Obispo, CA 93401, www.ladeda-online.com. This is a wonderful shop specializing in old furniture pieces and home decorating accents. I want to thank the three wonderful ladies of the shop – Sandy Howe, Pattea Torrence and Judy Watkins, for introducing me to several of their clients who were gracious in allowing us to photograph their homes.

Credits:
Lines on page 13 quoted from "For Friends Only," W.H. Auden in *Selected Poetry of W.H. Auden*, (New York: Random House, 1970).

Table of Contents

The prospect of entertaining overnight guests can be both thrilling and chilling – something most of us approach with a mix of anticipation and hesitation, something we wish we could do more easily and comfortably. That's where this book comes in. We begin by offering helpful advice from innkeepers at two successful country inns, and then we provide numerous examples of how to put their ideas – and more – into practice.

The physical space of the guest room can be as simple and small as a convertible sofa in your family room or a daybed in your home office, or it might be as elaborate and spacious as a suite of rooms or an entire wing of your house. Quite possibly, it's a separate room you use only occasionally. We've included ideas for furnishing, decorating, and outfitting many types of guest rooms, with numerous examples and tips and lots of lovely photographs.

Entertaining, when all is said and done, is more about grace than space. So we've included tips and recommendations for pampering your guests, identifying both essential elements and thoughtful touches that can make visits memorable and remind your guests just how special they are. We've chosen some wonderful recipes from the menus of country inns and listed suggestions for delicious, people-pleasing breakfasts and refreshing afternoon snacks.

We hope you enjoy your time with us.

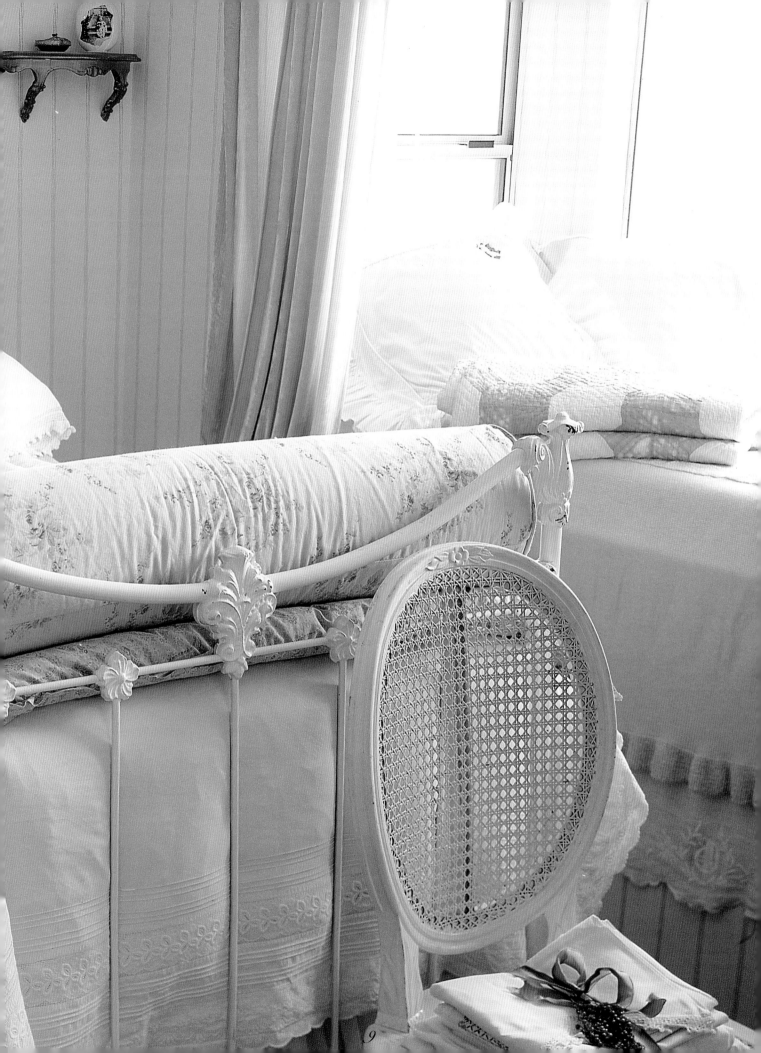

Secrets from Country Inns

You can learn a lot about entertaining guests from innkeepers – people whose business it is to provide their guests with a welcoming atmosphere and a pleasant experience. We've asked advice from two innkeeping couples: Barrie and Bobby Aycock, who own and operate the Glen-Ella Springs Inn in Clarkesville, Georgia and De and Mike Kennedy, who own and operate the Five Gables Inn in East Boothbay, Maine. In this section we present their tips and ideas – the hospitality and decorating secrets that have aided their success.

The ornament of a house is the friends who frequent it.
RALPH WALDO EMERSON

Glen-Ella Springs
A RUSTIC COUNTRY INN

The Perfect Guest Room

Tips from Barrie Aycock, innkeeper

The British poet and dramatist W. H. Auden wrote a poem he called "For Friends Only" for my brother and his wife, John and Teckla Clark, whom he often visited at their home in the Tuscan hills near Florence. It begins like this:

> Ours yet not ours, being set apart
> As a shrine to friendship,
> Empty and silent most of the year,
> This room awaits from you
> What you alone, as visitor, can bring,
> A weekend of personal life.

I love his idea of this room set apart as a "shrine to friendship." To me this poem expresses the perfect setting for a guest room, a place where one feels perfectly at home, whether it's the first visit, or the tenth.

I want a comfortable room, clean and fresh, with plenty of good pillows, but not so many that there's no room left on the bed for me. (Many people are allergic to goose down, so if that's what you have, make sure you have some synthetic spares, just in case.) A good reading lamp by the bed, and space on the table for my stuff is important. I love to lie in bed and read, but my other half wants a comfortable chair. I want a clock, set to the correct time. I don't especially want to hear your telephone, so unplug the one in my room unless it's a separate line. Make room in the closet for my things; a drawer or two of my own in the chest is a luxury if I'm staying for several days. If I'm living out of the suitcase, please give me a low table or a luggage stand to put my suitcase on so I'm not tripping over it the whole time. A favorite book of short stories and a few current magazines are thoughtful touches. Of course, a fresh new plant or some cut flowers would be lovely.

Our guests don't always like to sleep at the same temperature we do; an individual heat control in the guest room would be a luxury. A window that opens is heaven to me. I have one friend in Florida who keeps her house like a refrigerator in the summer. I close my door at night, open the windows, and am happy as a clam. Please always have a blanket or two on the shelf for cold-natured guests.

Continued on next page

Continued from page 13

In the bathroom, if there's a pedestal sink, please have a table nearby for our toiletries, good lighting for applying my makeup, and a full-length mirror on the door. A drinking glass and tissues are two more essentials. Don't forget a spare roll of toilet paper and a plunger for temperamental new-age plumbing. A bottle of aspirin and some antacid tablets might be very much appreciated after too much dinner and good wine. Take a basket and fill it with small amenities and toiletry samples you can buy at the store in case I forgot my razor, toothbrush, shampoo, or lotion. A sewing kit can be a lifesaver, as can a Band-Aid or two.

To give your guest room the supreme test, be a guest in it yourself for a night. Check out the shower. Is the water pressure strong enough? Look at that shower curtain. Does it stay in the tub, and is it free of mildew? Is there a non-skid mat on the floor? Are there hooks or racks to hang wet towels? How about the tub? Does the stopper work so I can soak in a hot bath? Is there good lighting near the tub, as well as over the sink or vanity? Is there room for my things in the drawer, or is it still full of your daughter's makeup that she left when she went off to college? Let common sense dictate. Less often is better than more in a guest room.

Auden ended his poem with: *Felicissima notte!* (Italian for "delighted night"). It's a lovely wish for a good night's rest. ❑

Five Gables Inn

A Coastal Bed and Breakfast

A Personal Touch

Tips from De Kennedy, inkeeper

There is nothing more personal than having someone in your home, and creating attractive, comfortable, and comforting guest rooms is a prime pleasure at Five Gables Inn. We consider innkeeping to be one of the few professions left that provides something on the human scale in a corporate world. It's about anticipating your guests' needs ahead of time, and it is very satisfying. It provides the opportunity to pay your guests the highest compliment – to cater to their needs and comfort.

The first tip (and I think the most important one)

I offer is this: Before even beginning to decorate, sleep in your guest room. (We have slept in each of the 16 guest rooms in our inn.) It is the only way you can be sure the bedside reading lamp is good and the mattress is truly comfortable. Check out what you actually see when your head is on the pillow, and find out how well the shower is draining.

In general, keep your decor simple and clutter free. Select your main color and pick it up throughout the room. Think light and airy. Beadboard wainscoting is a great look – you can buy it in sheets ready to install. Paint it white and paint the wall

Continued on page 18

Continued from page 16

above it a soft color. If your wall to wall carpeting is looking less than perfect and you do not want to replace it yet, a couple of lightweight, washable throw rugs can look quite nice on top of it.

Be sure to leave plenty of space on tables for your guests to put their own things. Knick-knacks and collectibles work best on mantels and shelves, out of the way. If you are lucky enough to have a pretty view from your guest room keep the window treatments simple. Our rooms have water views so we keep curtains to a minimum and have pull down shades for privacy.

Since we are located on the coast of Maine, we lean towards the "Maine cottage" look – wainscoting, crisp blues and whites, window seats, and (always!) light, airy, un-fussy rooms. Once the basics are taken care of, you can start the fun stuff. I call it "poofing." I like to put unexpected, whimsical touches in our rooms. In a room that has some high shelves I painted a few little flowers on the underside of one shelf. They are only seen from the bed when your head is on the pillow. On the inside of one closet door, I painted vines trailing around the full length mirror that is attached to the inside of the door. In a room that has a country look, I painted the outside of the closet door red, like a barn door.

Above a bed in another room I attached a board

with five pegs. (These are easy to find in stores and can be painted to match the room.) Hanging from it are a string shopping bag with a few shells, a blue glass ball, an antique coat hanger, and a little woven antique purse. I like tiny vases of flowers or a couple

of seashells on window sills. New drawer pulls can really change the look of an old dresser, especially one you've painted. I love the retro-looking green and clear glass ones.

I have a friend who decorates one of her guest room walls with framed photos of her "regulars" who stay in the room. It's fun to go in and see your picture on the wall. Real homey. On the bed she has a pillow that says, "There's No Friends Like Old Friends." That always seems like such a welcoming touch to me. ❏

Creating a Guest Room

A guest room can be a visual extension of your home's decor or a place apart, somewhere you can create drama, add luxury, and indulge fantasy. It doesn't need to be the place to store castoff ugly furniture and mismatched odds and ends.

The rooms featured in this section are wonderful examples of memorable, comfortable guest rooms. They showcase an assortment of furnishings and color schemes and vary widely in size, color, and cost. Some are simple, others ornate. Some are cozy, and some are grand. Some are tiny, some are spacious. There's something to learn in each one. Use them to glean ideas for making your guest room a comfortable haven, the kind of place you'd like to visit.

Good Thoughts

Roses – the flower that symbolizes affection – and words – Hope ... Love ... Peace ... Charity ... Faith ... Joy – are the inspiration for this guest room designed by Susan Goans Driggers for Plaid Enterprises, Inc. The words are stenciled on a painted wooden headboard that's joined to a simple foundation constructed of 2 x 4 lumber and cabinet grade plywood. Subtly stenciled letters form a textured background on the bed and on an uplifting border at door-top height that's punctuated with colorful roses. A tone-on-tone effect is achieved on the wall by adding stenciled words in lower case letters to the green stripes above the horizontal border. A rose motif quilt and ruffled and tasseled pillow shams dress the bed and extend the floral theme. "Love" is stenciled on a square pillow.

Stenciling Supplies and Tips

You can stencil designs on walls, furniture, and fabrics, creating a custom look with the colors of your choosing.

SUPPLIES

To create a stenciled room, you need stencils, paint, and applicators. Pre-cut stencils in a variety of styles and motifs are available at crafts stores and home improvement centers, where you'll also find paints and gels in myriad colors that are especially made for stenciling. To stencil, you pounce or swirl paint through the cutout openings of the stencil with a flat-tipped bristle brush, a sponge applicator, a small roller, or a sponge.

TIPS

• Stenciling is a "dry brush" painting technique, one that uses very little paint. Most mistakes are made from having too much paint on the brush or applicator.

• Practice stenciling on a piece of wood or poster board before working on a wall or furniture.

• Before you stencil letters, it's a good idea to copy the stencil pattern on a copy machine and loosely cut out the shapes. Position the cutouts on the areas and tape them in place to try them out. Step back to judge the placement, and adjust until the result pleases you. Then you're ready to stencil.

• Stores that sell stenciling supplies often provide demonstrations or classes in stenciling techniques. You can also find numerous books devoted to the subject in libraries and stores.

• If you don't want to tackle the project yourself, hire a professional to stencil for you.

White Light

White is bright, clean, and soothing. In this airy room, white paint gives a unified, coordinated look to a collection of flea market finds. Note the variety of interesting shapes, such as the scalloped trim on the bedside pedestal table and the arched, ornamented headboard on the four-poster bed. A white enameled pitcher holds a bouquet of white flowers; the pitcher-and-basin set on the dresser echoes the shape.

In an otherwise all-white space, small touches of color draw the eye. In this uncluttered room, the antique blue and white quilt on the bed is the centerpiece. A guest room is a wonderful place to display and use more fragile linens, such as vintage quilts and lacy pillow shams, that might not hold up to the rigors of daily service.

Tropical Warmth

Coral walls, exotic flowers arranged with bamboo stalks, and a bamboo-framed mirror over a simple painted chest evoke the warmth of the tropics in this guest room. Bird-motif china plates, the black dresser, and other black accents stand out from the vivid wall color, adding contrast and drama. The porcelain parrot in a vintage birdcage is a whimsical touch.

Twin beds, placed together, provide sufficient separation for guests who might prefer not to share a bed, such as unrelated individuals, adult siblings, or children, but are close enough for a couple. Matching vintage cotton chenille bedspreads were the inspiration for the wall color. The tropical-print pillow shams and reed window blinds recall Florida in the 1950s. A colorful quilt at the foot of the bed invites an afternoon nap.

Arts and Crafts

This small room is a restful retreat with ample natural light, a comfortable bed with plenty of pillows, and a bouquet of lilies on the dresser. Even though the room is small, it contains all that is needed to make a guest comfortable. The early 20th century oak dresser provides a place for guests to store clothing and other essentials. A wooden chair provides a resting place for a basket of rolled terry towels and washcloths and a fresh bar of soap.

A wicker lamp base, shown at left and below, extends the light, airy feeling. The handmade paper shade is decorated with dried, pressed leaves. A thoughtfully chosen selection of books rests between brass bookends, inviting a bedtime read.

Homey and Homemade

A guest room is the perfect place to display and make use of handmade furnishings – ones you make yourself, pieces made by family members, or favorite craft fair finds.

The room pictured on the opposite page exemplifies how appealing hand-painted and home-made can be. The blue-painted bed with a distressed finish was created by Susan Goans Driggers for Plaid Enterprises, Inc. The acrylic paint was sanded to create a time-worn look. The pedestal table is an unfinished piece of furniture that was painted with acrylic paints to match the colors of the quilt. The cheery colors of the patchwork coverlet, tufted with fabric-covered buttons, are

echoed in the crocheted and braided handmade rug. The black accents in the rug's borders are repeated in the checked border of the table and the framed pictures. A grouping of old-fashioned chenille pillows adds to the comfort.

In the bedroom shown below, a plethora of patterns, including stripes, checks, and floral prints, are happily combined. The circus motif of the pillow sham print and the golden stars on the skirted bedside table are lighthearted touches. A white cotton bedspread and a pieced patchwork comforter dress this bed that is fitted with a painted and distressed headboard. A good reading light is a must in any guest room.

Rustic Elegance

The elegant furnishings and fabrics of this guest suite at Glen-Ella Springs Inn are a pleasing contrast to the rustic wood paneling. The richly patterned rug and floral print of the chair upholstery are warm and inviting. The white matelasse coverlet and lace-trimmed pillowcases balance the two-toned print used for the comforter, bedskirt, and pillow shams and the striped accent pillows. Botanical prints in gold frames are another elegant touch. Simple wide-slat wood-toned blinds open to let in lots of light and blend with the walls when closed.

Grand Style

Thanks to its soaring height and angled placement, this four-poster mahogany bed occupies center stage. The dark wood furniture, ornate gold picture frames, and the symmetrical arrangement of the pillows on the bed are elements that establish a formal look. Even though this is a small room, the large furniture makes it look opulent, not cramped.

A gold framed mirror fills the wall above a low dresser, expands the space, and balances the tall window. Leaning it, rather than hanging, makes it look less formal. Paired lamps, inspired by classical urns, provide light for reading on either side of the bed. A pair of porcelain monkey statues flank a small painting on an easel. A green plant adds life to the room.

Chocolate, Vanilla, and Mint

Here's a guest room with a color scheme that's good enough to eat! One color – a refreshing mint green – is used for the walls and the plaid fabric on the skirted table. Everything else in the room is neutral – a chocolate brown coverlet, large-scale brown and white gingham checked pillows and bedskirt, brown toile print ruffled shams and draperies, a pale beige carpet. Who said not to mix checks and plaids? Here it works.

The accessories are in the British Colonial style and add a classical, yet informal atmosphere to the room. The bed is of bronze-toned metal bed with a padded leather headboard., Classic inspired urn-shaped lamps with simple white shades flank the bed to provide ample lighting. The framed mirror and prints with monkey motifs are stylish accents that pull this look together.

Thoughtfully, the hosts have kept surfaces clear, provided drawer space and a picture book for perusing, and placed a metal framed alarm clock at the bedside.

Cozy Nooks

Architectural features such as gable windows and slanted ceilings, common to second-story and attic rooms, and small rooms where space is limited present decorating challenges. The solutions? Sleek built-ins that pair seating and storage for double duty in guest rooms.

Here, a guest room gable houses a window seat with a drawer for storage built underneath. The upholstered pillow on top provides seating for reading and relaxing, and pillows in a variety of sizes and patterns can be re-arranged to suit. A light fixture in the peak of the gable ensures illumination; a narrow shelf above the window displays collectibles. The window seat could also be used as sleeping space for a child.

Because of the slanted ceiling, wall space is scarce. Drawers built under the bed make a chest unnecessary and contribute to the light, airy feeling of the room.

The water view from the gable window in this room at the Five Gables Inn was the inspiration for this room's blue color scheme. Two tones of soothing light blue were used on the walls. On the line where the two colors meet, the words, "by the sea, by the sea, by the beautiful sea" are repeated all around the room, painted in white. A built-in window seat with an upholstered cushion provides seating and storage. Nautical stripes and ship motifs are used for cushion covers; a needlepoint pillow literally invites guests to relax.

Another sea-inspired room takes its color cues from the tints of seashells. This similar space gains a very different look and feel with off-white paint in the gable, a collection of pillows trimmed in vintage lace and crochet on the window seat, and a view-of-the-sea mural painted on the walls next to the bed.

Sleek built-ins and lots of white paint make the most of the space in this room. A twin-size mattress rests on a platform above a row of drawers. By day, with layers of arranged pillows, it's a cozy place to sit, nap, or curl up with a book. Remove the pillows, and it's a place for another guest to sleep. An adjacent ledge is a convenient place for a lamp.

Having a wall fixture next to the bed keeps the bedside table clear for a clock radio and reading material. The wall switch is within easy reach. Above the beadboard wainscoting, narrow shelves built as cubbyholes hold interesting arrangements of books, china, collectibles, and dried flowers.

Red and white make a cheery combination in this upstairs guest room – a pieced coverlet with cross-stitch trim, pillow covers and cafe curtains stitched from a variety of red and white tea towels, and a tapestry pillow. Stenciled cherries form a border that accents the slanted wall behind the bed.

Collections on Display

A guest room that's out of the main traffic pattern of your household can provide the perfect spot for displaying prized collectibles – they're safely stored but out in view, not out of sight. Your guests will feel very special to be entrusted with your treasures.

In this room, a pine shelf placed above a pine chest between the beds holds a collection of green majolica plates and ceramic rabbits. The chest is a creative diversion from using two bedside tables. On the bureau top, a collection of candlestick lamps keep company with other china pieces. Rabbit motifs also are evident in the framed painting, the lamp, and the cachepot on the glass-topped metal table beside a chair.

The calm green wall paint and the British Colonial print draperies provide most of the color; the white matelasse coverlets, ecru throws, beige carpeting, and light wood tones are restful neutral shades.

British Colonial

Cool green is spiced with burnt orange and accented with black in this twin-bedded room. Here, because of space constraints, the decorator chose to place the beds in front of the windows, framing the headboards with the print draperies. The look is symmetrical and appealing. The horizontal lines of the window shutters balance the strong verticals of the bed posts, lamps, and draperies. A black wicker table between the beds holding lamps, books, and a clock can be reached from either bed.

Tall windows, above, frame a garden view and create a sunny alcove for reading, visiting, and relaxing. The swagged bright print fabric draws the eye upward; other furnishings in the room are purposefully low. Using the same woven fabric for the bedcover, most of the pillows, and the chair and ottoman upholstery gives a unified, custom look and soothes the eye. The bare walls are a restful background.

An armoire can serve many purposes in a guest room — providing the hanging and storage space of a closet in a room without one or concealing a television set or a computer. The crackled finish on this one is a textured variation of the wall color.

Palm trees, tropical bird prints in gilded frames, and an exotic-theme print used for tasseled draperies and fringed pillows create a rich-looking room. The iron frame bed is focal point; curtains and canopy are left to the imagination. The metal bench adds welcome curves and is a handy spot for placing suitcases and tote bags.

Pastel and Pretty

Pastel colors evoke the warmth and light of summer in any season but are, paradoxically, cooling. Combining pastels with generous amounts of white – in painted trim, furniture, window coverings, or bedding – keeps things from looking fussy.

In this room, the grid-design wallpaper imparts a subtle color and texture to the walls. Botanical-themed accessories – a flower-trimmed straw hat hung on the wall above the bed, floral-motif prints on pillows, and a bouquet of fresh flowers on the table – bring the beauty of the summer garden indoors.

A Plush Purple Palace

A room of pale pastels – lavender, peach, and white – takes on a winter coziness with the addition of purple velvet drapery panels and a plaid woven throw in shades of sage, beige, and purple. When spring comes around again, replace the velvet panels with white lace and trade the woven throw for a small patchwork quilt or a lightweight crocheted afghan.

Leaves and Fishes

Botanical print fabrics and an array of fish-motif designs that express the interests of the hosts are linked by a common color – moss green. The biggest expanse of solid green is seen in the draperies; smaller touches are evident in the picture mat, a painted Shaker-style wooden box, and a painted wooden chair. The straw pith helmet is a sporty touch. While the dresser is pickled white, it's top is given a bright accent – a red crackled finish top.

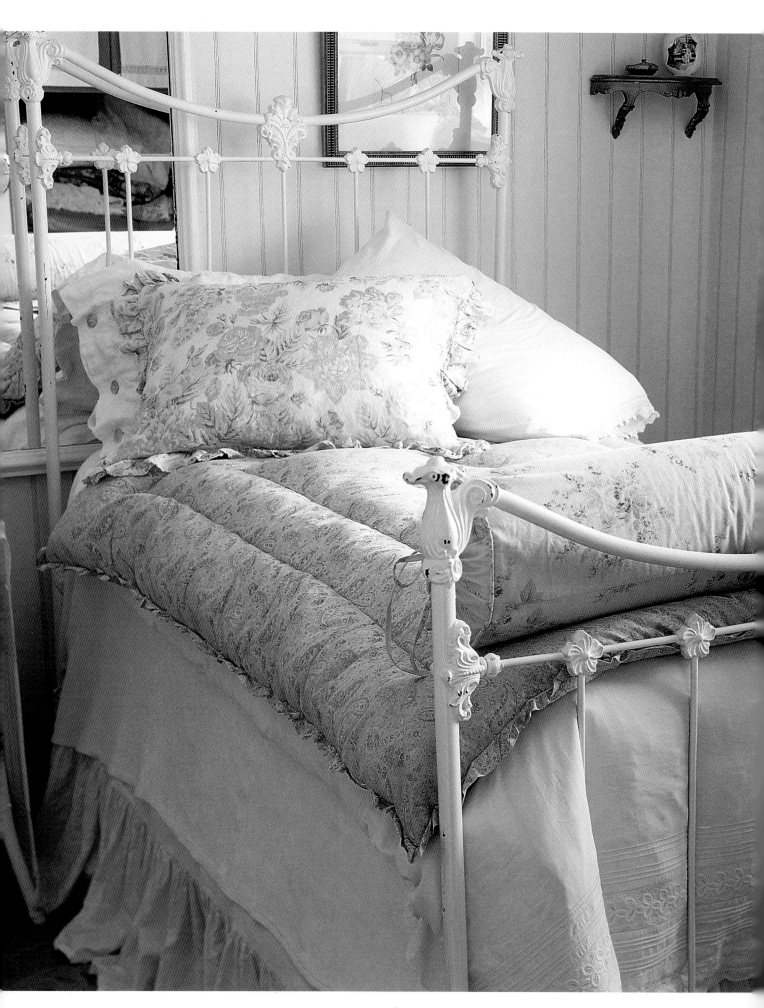

Sunshine and Flowers

This sunny room has two sleeping spaces – the ornate iron bedstead, outfitted with layers of linens and topped with a feather-bed and casually arranged pillows, and a twin size bed created on the large window seat. Decked out with ruffled shams and an antique quilt worn from years of use makes it most inviting. Sheer curtains shield the main part of the room from bright light and create a separate room within the room for the guest sleeping in the alcove. This would be a perfect room for a couple sharing a room with their young child or three little girls having a slumber party.

Converting a Room

If you have room in your heart, but not in your home, for overnight guests, you can entertain them in style even if you don't have a separate room devoted to that purpose.

A room that does double duty is a fine option when space is limited, if you infrequently have guests who spend the night, or for those times when the number of guests you're hosting exceeds the capacity of your guest room.

Though visiting children (or your own offspring, if their rooms are needed for guests) may enjoy sleeping on a pallet of quilts on the floor or an inflatable mattress in the den or even a night or two in a sleeping bag in a tent in the backyard, most of us (if the truth be told) require a little more in the way of creature comforts. On the other hand, if your city is hosting the Olympics or you live in an area that's a prime business or pleasure destination and you're happy having people underfoot from time to time, offer what you can and know your guests will be grateful.

In the artful examples that follow, you'll see how it's possible to marry high tech with high touch and easily transform sitting and working spaces into sleeping spaces. And vice versa. The same attributes that make a room the perfect daytime retreat or home office – privacy, quiet, separation – also make it a good guest room come nightfall.

Here, the part of this room used for the office is so charming guests wouldn't mind that the room does double duty. They may even want to take advantage of the technology by picking up their email. Antique chairs with floral print fabrics and a charming armoire to hold office supplies are pretty enough for guests, yet functional when it comes time for this room to get down to business.

Sitting Room

Most days, this sitting room serves as a restful daytime or evening retreat. The wonderful black mantel is an elegant focal point, and the wicker armchair next to the hearth is a cozy sitting spot. The daybed, used in lieu of a sofa, takes up less visual space than a sofa of comparable size, and is great for stretching out with a good book, a brand new magazine, or the Sunday paper or for catching an afternoon nap. Because it's a twin-size bed, the daybed – with the addition of sheets and pillowcases – can become a comfortable place for an overnight guest.

Computer Hideaway

What's in this armoire? With its doors closed, you might think it's an armoire or linen press, filled with stored out-of-season clothing or bed linens. But when the doors open, customized shelving is revealed that holds a computer monitor and keyboard, office supplies, CPU, and (higher up) a compact stereo system and CDs. Voila! A complete home office.

An armless chair, upholstered in a floral print on the seat and in a coordinating stripe on the back, is an unusual but serviceable workstation seat that belies its utilitarian function.

Window Seat Conversion

Home office? Sleeping space? Sitting room? It all depends on the time of day and the situation. This room does triple duty – beautifully. At left, customized cabinets hold computer, fax, and office supplies. Under the windows, the cabinets are the base for a window seat designed as a sleeping space for a guest. Shutters provide privacy when the need arises.

On the following pages, the sitting room (or maybe it's the conference room?) is revealed. The seats of a pair of French provincial armchairs are draped in white linen and lace. A glass-topped weathered metal table comes in from the garden to hold flowers, a topiary, and a lamp. Stacks of magazines act as risers. Under the table, a crackle-finish rabbit statue – another garden touch – rests on an upholstered ottoman.

Home Office

This home office has a hidden second life, cleverly concealed in a wall that also includes cabinets, shelves, and pull-out drawers for holding files. By day – most days – it's a sleek, elegant workspace. But when the occasion arises (as you'll see on the following pages), a full-size bed drops down and a comfortable guest room emerges. Designed by furniture maker Bill Thomsen and built by Thomsen Ltd., the wall unit is a striking example of the advantages of a customized approach.

ABOVE: With the bed pulled down and the computer printer put away, the room is ready to welcome guests. Bath towels are folded on a shelf. A child's quilt, hung on the wall behind the bed, adds color and occupies minimal space. Pull-out shelves on either side of the bed make convenient night tables.

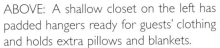

ABOVE: A shallow closet on the left has padded hangers ready for guests' clothing and holds extra pillows and blankets.

LEFT: The rolling cart (another Thomsen design) can hold suitcases in the guest room configuration or the computer's printer in the office. A shelf in the cart is just the right height for a slim-profile photocopier. For more information about Thomsen's designs, see the "Acknowledgements" section at the front of the book.

Executive Guests

This room is a comfortable den most days, with a mission-style futon sofa for lounging and shelving for books, displays of memorabilia, and photos. A slim desk modeled on a mission-style library table holds a laptop computer and doubles as a home office. A rice-paper shoji screen shields the space from the room beyond.

The neutral walls and floor-covering are a restful backdrop for lively colors – a soft purple slipcover and turquoise and bronze silk noil pillows with shiny piping. But a few simple modifications convert the space into a cozy retreat for overnight guests. To see how, turn the page.

ABOVE: The back of the sofa folds down to make a full-size bed. Brown-print sheets and pillowcases and a coordinating comforter are restful and inviting. The desk chair becomes a place to put a book.

OPPOSITE PAGE: Brown chenille-covered pillows, at top, provide additional support for reading in bed. The lamp provides ample light. Below, a sleek alarm clock in a wooden case joins the lamp and the carved wooden animals. With the computer put away, there's plenty of space on the desk for an earthenware pitcher of water, a pair of drinking glasses, and the newspaper.

Ways to Pamper Your Guests

Think of the times you've stayed in a hotel, an inn, or someone's home. What made you feel at home and pampered? In this section we explore the thoughtful details and welcoming touches that contribute so much to your guests' comfort, safety, and pleasure.

"In our rooms at Five Gables Inn," says innkeeper De Kennedy, "we include written information that will be helpful to our guests. The same thing can be done in a home. This information is especially helpful if you are at work during the day and not available to entertain your guests. Include restaurant recommendations with phone numbers, brochures of local attractions, practical notes about your home (such as information about the washer and dryer, where you keep the coffee, and how to use the coffeemaker), and your phone number at work in case they need to contact you.

"Keep this stored in your computer so you can use it again for your next guests. Print it out on pretty paper and add a handwritten note that welcomes your guests and ends with something like, 'Have a great day. See you tonight at 7 for cocktails and dinner.'"

Here are other ideas for furnishing and enhancing your guest room:

• Put sachets in a few of the dresser drawers and in the closet.

• A small desk is nice if you have the space – it can double as a dressing table if you put a makeup mirror on it.

• If you place a decanter of water and a glass by the bed, guests won't need to wander around looking for a drink. Decanters with a matching glass turned over the top take up little space.

• Place a guidebook to your area and a good street map in the room.

• In a basket or drawer, place a few postcards of the area, some writing paper and envelopes, and a few stamps. (This last may be the most thoughtful of all, since it's usually not easy to locate a post office in an unfamiliar place.)

• Keep a flashlight next to the bed in case the power goes out.

• Provide a night light, one that's easy to switch off. Some people don't like to sleep without a night light; others can't bear any light at all for sleeping.

• A full length mirror in the guest room is a great convenience. It can be hung on the inside of the closet door (the best place) or on a wall or on the back of the door to the room.

Blankets and Pillows

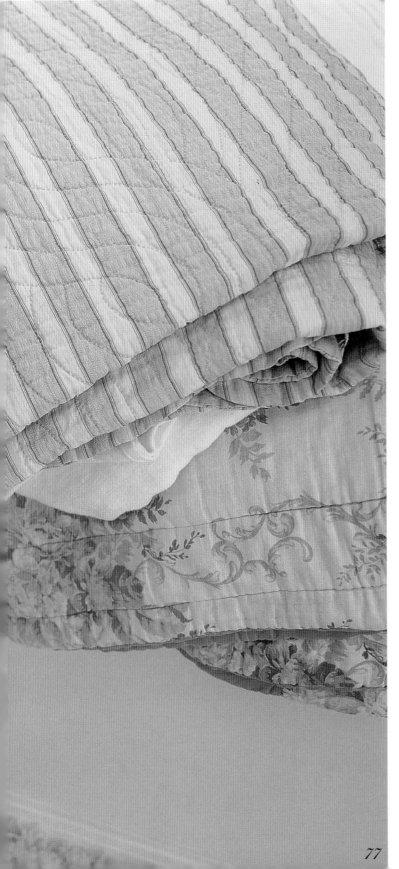

Whatever the weather, some people like to cover up, so be sure to have extra blankets on hand – light quilts or cotton coverlets in warmer weather, woolen or acrylic or thermal blankets or comforters in winter. You can fold them at the foot of the bed, stack them on a shelf, or hang them over a chair. Think of them as colorful, moveable, changeable elements of your decor.

Blankets, comforters, and throws make people feel comfortable and cozy. A stack of patchwork quilts is lovely to look at, evokes nostalgia, and invites reminiscences.

Put four bed pillows on a full-size (or larger) bed or two on each twin bed so people who want to read in bed can be comfortable. Decorative throw pillows look great on a bed, but resist the temptation to get carried away – at bedtime, your guests may find it a hassle to deal with them.

Be considerate of people with allergies – not everyone can use down quilts or pillows, so be sure to have hypoallergenic ones, too.

 Linens

Buy the best sheets you can afford – 100% cotton (plain or damask weave) or linen are best. For a really luxurious feel, buy the highest thread count of cotton sheets that you can afford. The thread count denotes the number of lines of yarn woven into a square inch of fabric. Resist buying sheets of polyester blends. Sheets with higher thread counts are softer and have better durability. The "luxury" category usually starts with 200 thread count. You won't believe how wonderful 350 thread count Egyptian cotton sheets feel. Yes, the type of cotton also makes a difference. Egyptian cotton is considered the finest cotton for bed linens. Next in line is pima cotton which is a long fiber cotton. The majority of sheets you find are percale, which is a tight, plain weave fabric. These linens are fine as long as you buy anything above 180 or 200 thread count. Wash and dry them several times in lightly scented or unscented detergent to make them extra soft. Have at least two sets for each bed, and be sure they're spotlessly clean.

If you live in a cold climate, remember nothing is cozier than curling up in a bed with flannel sheets in the winter. (Some people use them all year.) And a flat flannel sheet makes a great lightweight blanket in the summer.

For variety and nostalgia, try using vintage pillowcases (ones trimmed with handmade lace or embroidery, for example) on some of your bed pillows. They're easy to find in secondhand shops and at tag sales. When not in use, vintage linens make a lovely display, at right, when folded and tied with a colorful ribbon and a spray of berries.

Solid-color bedspreads made of matelasse or chenille wash and dry easily, and you can dress them up with pillow shams in prints or stripes. For a coordinated look, use the fabric of the shams to slipcover a chair or make a small throw pillow or seat cushion.

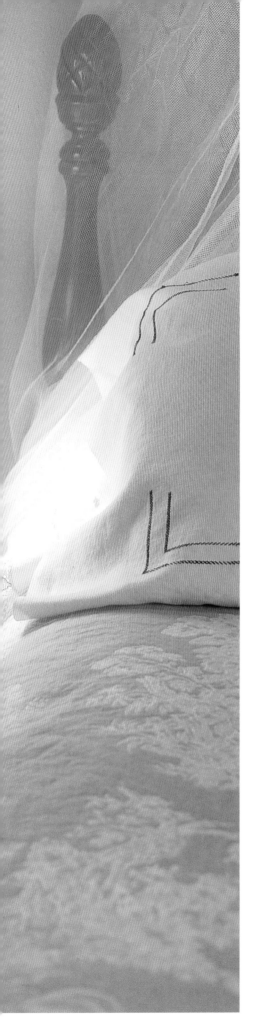

Wake Up Call

It's a good idea to inform your guests about your routine, especially if you will be going to work, getting kids off to school, or singing in the choir on Sunday morning while they are visiting you. Likewise, be sure you are aware of any commitments they have made for the time of their visit and schedules they need to keep for meetings, conferences, guided tours, or sightseeing attractions.

Encourage independence and autonomy by furnishing your guest room with an easy-to-operate alarm clock. A clock radio with an alarm is a welcome touch; so is a programming guide to radio stations in your area. If the clock is battery-powered, check the batteries. Be sure all clocks are set to the correct local time.

The clock on the bedside table, left, has an easy-to-read, luminescent face. The top drawer of the night table holds a box of tissues. An assortment of reading material is close at hand.

Restful Reading Retreat

Being away from home is an ideal time to catch up on one's reading or to take time to snuggle up with a good book. Because many people enjoy reading in bed, it's a good idea to have adequate pillows for reading and a lamp near the bed. Those who like to do their reading while sitting in a chair will appreciate having one available, whether it's a chaise longue or a chair-cum-ottoman combination like this one.

Have a lamp nearby that provides adequate light and, within easy reach, some clear space on a table to hold a cup or glass. A guest who forgot to pack reading glasses would no doubt appreciate the loan of a pair. One savvy hostess we know keeps an assortment of reading glasses in different strengths on hand just in case.

Fresh Flowers

Fresh flowers are a lovely, lively way to make a room look inviting and, well, fresh! Keep a selection of vases on hand in various sizes and heights. An unusual container, such as an ironstone pitcher or garden urn, can be charming.

Innkeeper De Kennedy calls fresh flowers "the very best decorating item." Unless your guest room is quite large, she advises, keep the arrangement simple and go for a "just picked from the garden" look. If you're not certain about your guests' allergies or sensitivities, steer clear of highly scented florals – you don't want to provoke a headache or sneezing. If the visit is longer than a few days, be sure to freshen the arrangement, change the water, and remove any spent blooms every day or two.

In the wintertime or if flowers just aren't available, substitute a flowering plant. Resist the temptation to add colorful flowers to a room by using artificial flowers. Most times they are simply dust collectors. Some beautiful ways to add fresh plants would be a poinsettia or Christmas cactus in bloom during winter holidays, a potted palm or orchid, or fresh-cut greens in a vase.

Unpacking

Most people don't like living out of a suitcase. The best way to make a guest feel welcome is to provide space in your home for their clothes and toiletries.

LUGGAGE STAND

Provide a stand for guests' luggage – it's a great convenience. They come in wood and metal and can be folded for storage when not in use.

If guests decide to unpack, the stand will help your furniture and fabrics stay clean by keeping dirty luggage off the bed and chairs. If they don't unpack, having a luggage rack handy raises the suitcase off the floor, eliminating back-breaking bending and allowing easy access.

If you don't have a "regulation" luggage stand, provide a bench or a wide, high stool. Any type of flat surface (a low chest, for example) that is sturdy and wide enough to hold the luggage and tall enough to keep your guests from having to bend over will work just fine.

This bench at the end of the bed, pictured above, usually holds extra blankets, but it can double as a place for guests' luggage or totes.

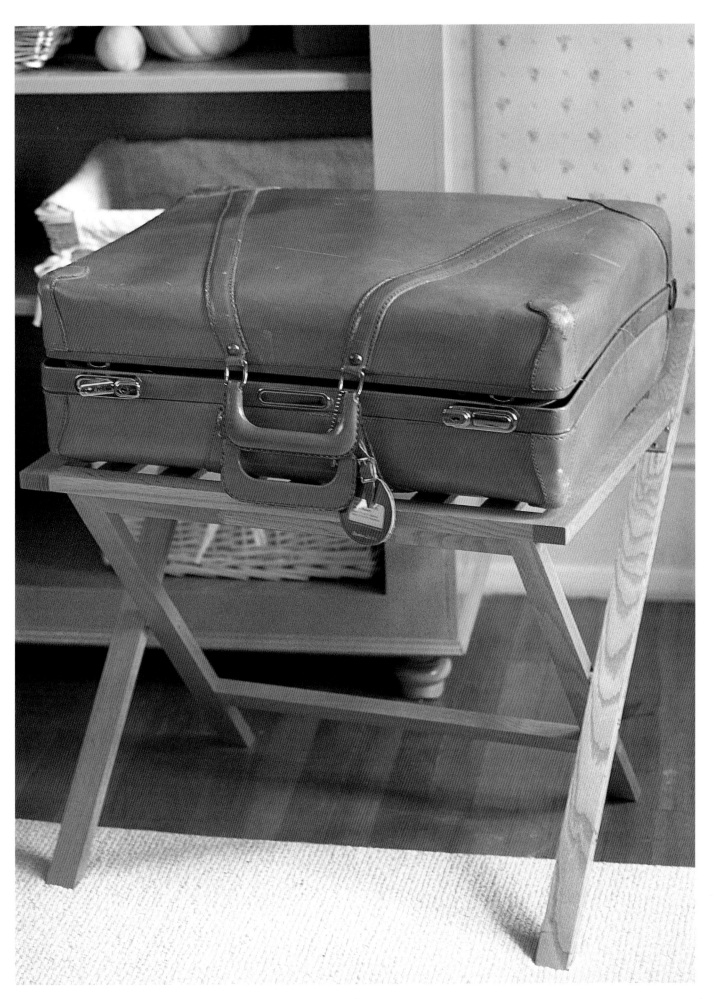

DRAWER AND CLOSET SPACE

Clean out a drawer or two in a chest in your guest room and let guests know there's drawer space for them to use. If drawer space is not available, pretty fabric-lined baskets on a shelf can be a charming alternative.

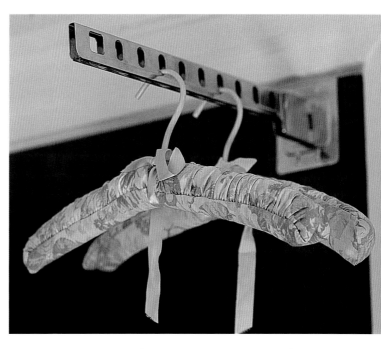

Make room in a closet for your guests to hang a few items, and supply some pretty padded hangers to make your guests feel special. If the room doesn't have a closet or you can't spare the space, provide an over-the-door portable rack. Simply hang it over any door to provide temporary space for hanging clothes.

SURFACES

You want your guest room to look homey and prettily decorated, but try to refrain from covering every surface. Allow some surfaces to remain free of decorative objects so guests will have a place to put toiletries, reading material, or other personal items.

SNACKS

Leaving a prepared snack in the room is a thoughtful touch. Fresh fruit is colorful, beautiful to look at, and delicious. Who can resist a small plate of cookies? Or a tin of mints, individually wrapped candies, a small box of gourmet chocolates, raisins or other dried fruit, or crackers?

For quenching thirst, have bottled water (both fizzy and still) and drinking glasses on hand. A nightcap – a decanter of sherry or port or a bottle of their favorite liqueur – is nice. Provide glasses for sipping on a tray. For those not wishing to drink alcohol, herbal teas are a welcome option.

TOILETRIES

Like well-run hotels do, you'll want to have toiletries available – shampoo, hand lotion, luxurious little soaps, a disposable razor, a shower cap. Travelers negotiating airport security may not have been able to bring nail clippers, nail files, or scissors and will be grateful you've supplied them.

You could also place a "notions basket" in the room. Include a travel-size sewing kit, a couple of buttons, some safety pins, and an extra light bulb. Put it in the top dresser drawer so guests will find it easily.

Sleeping Well

Here's how to help your guests get a good night's sleep.

AROMATHERAPY

Aromatherapy – the therapeutic use of essential oils distilled from plants – is a lovely way to promote relaxation and sleep. Essential oils believed to possess calming properties include lavender, clary sage, and rosewood. Other restful scents are vanilla, tangerine, and chamomile.

For a subtle sleep-inducer, sprinkle a few drops of lavender essential oil on a handkerchief or a piece of cotton and place it inside a pillowcase. Dried lavender, enhanced or refreshed with lavender essential oil, can be used to make closet or drawer sachets for your guest room.

Scented bath salts are easy to make and lovely to use. See the "Gifts for Your Guests" section for a recipe.

BATH HERBS

A warm bath is soothing and relaxing. To help your guests get a restful night's sleep after tiring days of traveling or busy days of sightseeing or meetings, brew a bath tea with this sleep-encouraging blend. Instructions for use follow the recipe.

MUSIC

Listening to music is another time-honored way to relax. "Music has charms to soothe a savage breast, To soften rocks, or bend a knotted oak," wrote playwright William Congreve in the 17th century. We agree.

Bath Herbs Recipe

Mix together in a bowl:
1 cup dried lemon verbena leaves
1/2 cup dried lavender buds
1/2 cup dried whole chamomile flowers
1/4 cup dried orange peel

Store in a glass jar or parchment envelope.

To package: Place 1/4 cup in a little fabric bag (make them yourself or buy muslin bags in herb shops or health food stores). For a more rustic presentation, place 1/4 cup herbs in a piece of cheesecloth, gather the ends together to form a pouch, and tie with twine.

To use: Simmer a bag on top of the stove in a pan with one quart of water for 10 minutes to make a fragrant "tea." Pour the tea and the bag in the bath water and relax. Use the wet bag to scrub and stimulate the skin. Discard after use. ❏

A way to listen to music, such as a radio or compact disc or tape player, is a thoughtful addition to a guest room.

Any kind of music can be relaxing, if it's a kind of music you enjoy. If you know your guests' tastes, whether they be rock, pop, easy listening, or hip hop, you can leave a note suggesting a radio station they would enjoy or provide CDs or tapes by their favorite artists. If you're not sure what they'd like, your best bets are light classics and instrumentals such as solo piano or acoustic guitar. Or try recorded sound effects intended for relaxation, ones with names like "seashore" or "rain," that help block extraneous sounds and promote relaxation.

Providing earphones or a headset is another nice touch.

BEVERAGES

A comforting cup of tea helps many people get a good night's sleep. Having a two-cup coffee maker or a small electric kettle (the kind that shuts itself off before it boils dry) available in the guest room is a thoughtful gesture. Supply decaf or herbal tea bags (chamomile, peppermint, and blends with names like Sleepytime, Calm, or Nighty Night are good choices). Don't forget cups, spoons, and sugar cubes or honey straws.

PAMPERING CHECKLIST

A list of items to have handy for guests to use in your home.

- Bottled water or water carafe or pitcher of water and glass
- Fresh flowers
- Snacks (fresh fruit, cookies, crackers, juice, tea)
- Extra blankets and pillows
- Alarm clock
- Hair dryer
- Toiletries and sewing notions
- Box of tissues
- Books related to your guests' interests or your locale
- Today's newspapers and recent magazines
- Reading lamp
- Flashlight
- Padded hangers
- Luggage rack
- One-size-fits-all bathrobe
- Electronic entertainment (radio, CD or tape player, small TV, perhaps a VCR or DVD player)
- Stationery, postcards, stamps
- Information about local attractions, restaurants, and transit
- Local map
- Folding breakfast tray (can double as a desk or reading table)

The Guest Bath

A separate guest bathroom is not a necessity, but it is a great convenience, one that allows your guests more of what everybody wants in a bathroom – privacy. If you or other members of your family will be sharing a bathroom with guests, you may need to confer about morning schedules and adjust wakeup times accordingly. To avoid confusion, place towels for your guests in their room and make it easy to identify towels by using different colors.

If you have a bathroom that's used exclusively for guests, be sure to try it out yourself to test its utility and comfort. Is everything easy to find? Is the mirror at a comfortable height? Is there enough light for shaving and applying makeup? Is there enough space on the sink or elsewhere to place a travel kit of toiletries?

How about the tub and/or shower? Is there space for placing soap, shampoo, conditioner within reach? Is there a bath mat? Hooks for hanging clothes or a robe? A place to hang a damp towel? When you recline in the tub, what do you see?

Is everything scrubbed and shiny? Have you provided air freshener? A scented candle or incense (and matches for lighting)? If there's a window, does the window treatment provide sufficient privacy? Resolve to correct any deficiencies you notice.

 Easy Access

Keeping items in plain sight makes life more convenient for everyone. Nobody wants to hunt through cupboards for a box of tissues and or a new roll of toilet paper. What constitutes an obvious storage place for you may not be so obvious to someone else.

For the same reason, don't make guests search for towels. Having extra clean ones available for use is a simple luxury, as is providing a washcloth for removing makeup. Below, an old iron bench with a velvet cover holds a basket of rolled towels in a guest bathroom. At right, a lace-trimmed hand towel hangs on a peg within easy reach of the sink. Oversized soap bars make an interesting sculptural display on the shelf.

Beautiful Bath Details

Stenciling creates a coordinated look in this sunny, spacious guest bathroom. A stylized leaf-and-flower border in muted greens and mauve-y pinks rings the room above the waist-high beadboard wainscoting. The same flowing motif is repeated at the top of the walls, emphasizing the slanted ceiling.

Motifs from the floral border are stenciled on a floor mat, above right, along with stylized dragonflies and bees. The wall border's floral motifs and the stylized dragonflies also adorn a painted wall shelf and a linen hand towel, left.

Floral stripes were created on the shower curtain by stenciling a narrow variation of the wall border design. A lush Boston fern on a low pedestal and flowers in a wall vase are fresh and vibrant.

Guest Towels

A guest bath is a great place to display and use beautiful towels that might not stand up to constant, repeated service, like the embroidered or lace-trimmed bath towels you couldn't resist or those lovely linen guest towels you inherited.

Here a wire basket beside the sink holds an eclectic collection of hand towels: sturdy terrycloth, lace-trimmed linen, embroidered cotton, fanciful applique. Interesting hand and guest towels, which are sometimes referred to as "finger towels," can be found at tag sales, flea markets, and secondhand shops and (probably) in the linen closets and attics of your relatives. Some may require ironing or special care; durability varies.

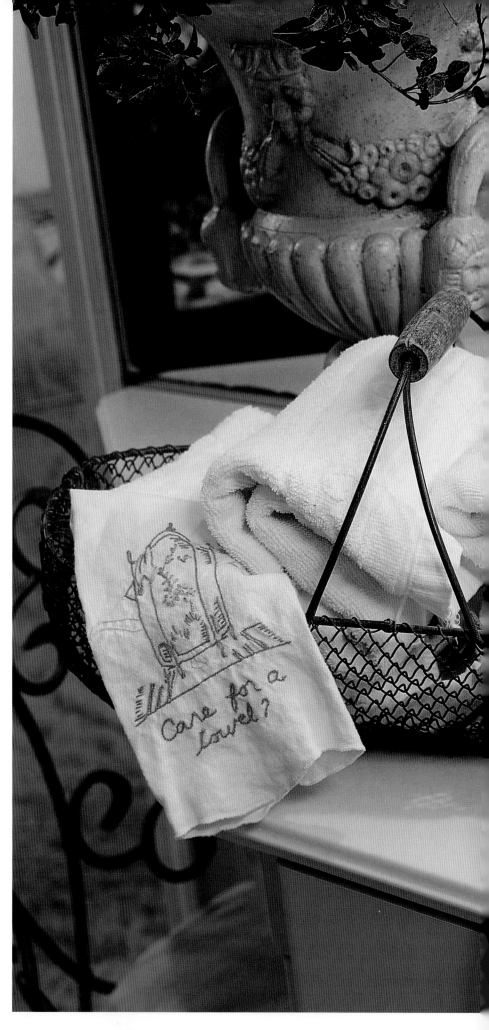

Special Touches

Though quite different in size and decor, these two bathrooms display the hosts' thoughtful attention to detail. The intense colors of the coral striped wall treatment and the deep green shower curtain, below, are balanced with the neutral tones of the floor, cabinet, and counter. Tissues in a crackle-finish box are easy to find. A china dish holds a selection of soaps. Coral terry towels are thoughtfully placed near the sink, on a chrome towel bar, and in a basket near the tub.

A large mirror and a neutral color scheme expands the look of a small space, right. Soaps, wrapped like gifts, are displayed in a glass dish. A white lace-trimmed towel is draped over a colored terry one on a wall-mounted brass ring. A pump bottle holds liquid hand soap; a small clock helps keep grooming rituals on schedule; a topiary in a painted pot brightens a corner. The small painting looms large and important when surrounded by an elaborate gold frame and hung in the small space. The lamp creates a warm glow.

Guests at Breakfast

Just about everybody wants to eat in the morning, but because "morning" doesn't necessarily mean the same time to everyone, be sure to inquire about your guests' plans and preferences or let them know yours by specifying a time and place. ("We have breakfast at 8:30 on the patio," for example.) There may be a divergence of opinion about what constitutes breakfast as well – some people are content with coffee, others want only fruit or a muffin or cereal, some need protein foods like eggs and bacon to start the day. Whatever the hour or food preference, serving your guests a breakfast you made especially for them is a lovely gesture.

If you're feeding a crowd, make a big breakfast casserole (some yummy recipes follow) so everyone can eat at once and together, even you! (Many breakfast casseroles can be assembled the night before and baked in the morning.) Or keep it simple and serve make-ahead breads and fruit with yogurt.

If you're entertaining more than a couple of guests and you're not sure everyone will want to eat at the same time, consider serving buffet style and choosing dishes that are good to eat whether they're piping hot, warm, or at room temperature, like a quiche or fritatta, or muffins, and baked or fresh fruit.

For one or two guests, you can be completely casual (bagels and cream cheese from the local deli or croissants from a bakery), cook something elaborate (Eggs Benedict or an omelet and orange juice fresh-squeezed in an antique press on the sideboard), or whip up a smoothie in the blender with fresh fruit, protein powder, and yogurt or soy milk.

On weekends, when things are more leisurely, take the time to set a pretty table (if you know you'll be pressed for time, you can do it the night before), with cloth napkins, fresh flowers, and sparkling glassware. During the week, when things may be more rushed, it only takes a moment to put juice or cream in a glass or pottery pitcher, serve the bread in a basket lined with a napkin, and put jam or jelly in a small bowl. It's so much more thoughtful and pleasant.

Breakfast at Five Gables Inn

Breakfast at the Five Gables Inn is a substantial meal that often features Maine favorites like blueberries and maple syrup or classics like Quiche Lorraine. The food is served buffet-style from a long hunt table in the inn's common room. A variety of egg dishes, sweets, veggies, breads, and muffins are prepared every day in the inn's kitchen. Familiar standbys like toast and boxed cereals with milk are also available along with juice, coffee, and tea.

Guests can seat themselves at long tables in the common room or (on sunny days) at smaller tables on the inn's veranda, where they can watch the boats on scenic Linekin Bay.

Ideas for Breakfast

- Muesli (oatmeal soaked overnight in yogurt and fruit juice, spiced with cinnamon, served with chopped apple, dried fruit, and nuts)
- Granola with fresh fruit and yogurt
- Scones
- Lemon Poppyseed Muffins or Morning Glory Muffins (recipes follow)
- Classics like Quiche Lorraine and Potatoes Anna
- Baked fruit (Blueberry Slump, Blueberry or Apple Crisp)
- Blueberry French Toast (recipe follows)
- Mushroom Crust Quiche (recipe follows)
- Bowl or platter of fresh fruit

Recipes from Five Gables Inn

Blueberry-Stuffed French Toast

6 to 8 servings

Innkeepers Mike and De Kennedy say this is their most-requested recipe. A perfect breakfast for those who enjoy something on the sweet side, the recipe works equally well with fresh or frozen blueberries. Assemble it the night before and bake just before serving, with Blueberry Sauce or maple syrup on top.

INGREDIENTS

12 slices French bread, 1" thick

2 8-ounce packages cream cheese

1 cup blueberries

12 eggs

1/3 cup maple syrup

2 cups milk

Butter

PROCEDURE

- Arrange half the bread slices in a buttered 9" x 13" glass baking dish. Cut up the cream cheese and scatter over the bread. Sprinkle blueberries over the cream cheese. Arrange remaining bread slices over blueberries.

- In a large bowl, whisk together the eggs, maple syrup, and milk. Pour the egg mixture evenly over the bread mixture and chill, covered, overnight.

- Preheat oven to 350 degrees. Remove covered dish from refrigerator and bake for 30 minutes. Remove foil. Bake 30 minutes more, until puffed and golden.

- While it bakes, make the Blueberry Sauce.

Blueberry Sauce

INGREDIENTS

1 cup sugar

2 tablespoons cornstarch

1 cup water

1 cup blueberries

1 tablespoon butter

PROCEDURE

In a small saucepan, stir together sugar, berries, cornstarch, and water. Cook over moderately high heat, stirring constantly, until berries have burst. Add butter. Stir until butter melts. ❑

Mushroom Crust Quiche

8 servings

This savory breakfast dish is a variation on a classic. The "crust" is unusual and delicious.

INGREDIENTS

5 tablespoons butter

1/4 cup finely chopped portobello mushrooms

3/4 cup fine dry bread crumbs

3/4 cup chopped green onions

2 cups shredded jack or cheddar cheese

6 eggs

1 cup cottage cheese

1/4 teaspoon paprika

1/4 teaspoon ground cayenne pepper

Non-stick cooking spray

PROCEDURE

- Preheat oven to 350 degrees.

- In a skillet over medium heat, melt 3 tablespoons butter. Add mushrooms. Cook until limp. Stir in bread crumbs. Coat pie plate with non-stick cooking spray. Press mixture evenly over the sides and bottom of pie plate.

- In the same skillet over medium heat, melt remaining 2 tablespoons butter. Add green onions and cook until limp. Spread onions over mushroom crust. Sprinkle evenly with shredded cheese.

- Place eggs, cottage cheese, and cayenne in the jar of a blender. Whir until smooth. Pour into prepared crust. Sprinkle with paprika. Bake 20 to 25 minutes. ❑

Lemon Poppy Seed Muffins

12 muffins

INGREDIENTS

3/4 cup sugar

3/4 cup butter, softened

1/2 teaspoon lemon extract

2 eggs, beaten

2 cups all-purpose flour

3 teaspoons baking powder

1/4 teaspoon ground nutmeg

1-1/4 cups milk

1/2 cup golden raisins

1/2 cup chopped walnuts

1/4 cup poppy seeds

Non-stick cooking spray

PROCEDURE

• Preheat oven to 400 degrees.

• In a bowl, cream together sugar, butter, and lemon extract. Beat in eggs.

• In a second bowl, combine flour, baking powder, and nutmeg. Add to the creamed mixture alternately with the milk, mixing until just blended.

• Fold in raisins, nuts, and poppy seeds. Coat 12 muffin cups or two 6-cup muffin tins with non-stick cooking spray. Spoon batter into muffin cups. Bake 20 minutes. ❏

Morning Glory Muffins

18 muffins

INGREDIENTS

1-1/4 cups sugar

2 cups all-purpose flour

2 teaspoons ground cinnamon

2 teaspoons baking soda

1/2 teaspoon salt

1/2 cup shredded coconut

1/2 cup raisins

1 cup shredded carrots

1 apple, cored and chopped

1/4 cup chopped pecans or walnuts

3 eggs, lightly beaten

1/2 cup vegetable oil

1/2 teaspoon vanilla extract

Non-stick cooking spray

PROCEDURE

• Preheat oven to 375 degrees.

• In a large bowl, sift together sugar, flour, cinnamon, baking soda, and salt.

• Add coconut, raisins, carrots, apple pieces, and nuts. Stir well.

• Add eggs, oil, and vanilla. Stir until just blended. coat muffin tins with non-stick cooking spray. Spoon batter into muffin cups. Bake 20 minutes. ❏

Breakfast at Glen-Ella Springs Inn

The menu at Glen-Ella Springs Inn changes daily, and many favorites have remained on the menu despite changes in chefs and staff. "I sample almost every new dish we prepare," says Barrie Aycock, "and I am the chefs' best and worst critic. My first love and favorite hobby had always been good food – eating, cooking, and just talking about it makes me happy."

BELOW: In your home you may want to set aside an area where your guests can help themselves to a morning beverage. This is especially helpful when you may have a full house during holidays or other special occasions. Here a cheery nook is set up with everything at hand for morning tea or coffee. Items are labeled with office supply store hang-tags for easy identification. Serving on a breakfront with open shelves makes everything easy to see and use.

Ideas for Breakfast

- After Easter Eggs (hardcooked eggs with cheese sauce)
- North Georgia stone ground grits (from the Logan Turnpike Mill in nearby Blairsville, Georgia)
- Scrambled Eggs with Cream Cheese and Basil
- Scrambled Egg Casserole (recipe follows)
- Spinach Quiche
- French Toast
- Banana Bread or Date Nut Prune Bread with Tangy Cream Cheese Spread (recipes follow)
- Corn Muffins or Apple Butter Muffins (recipe follows)
- Blintz Casserole (recipe follows)
- Granola (They make in large quantities and store in the freezer.)

Recipes from Glen-Ella Springs

Banana Bread

2 loaves (24 servings)

Barrie Aycock says this banana bread is very moist and freezes beautifully. The recipe makes two loaves – Barrie suggests you make both of them and put one in the freezer. You can defrost it as needed to make a delicious breakfast or snack for an unexpected guest.

INGREDIENTS

4 ounces butter, softened

2 cups sugar

4 eggs

2 teaspoons vanilla extract

3 cups flour

2 teaspoons baking soda

1/8 teaspoon salt

1 cup sour cream

3 cups mashed bananas

1 cup chopped pecans or walnuts

PROCEDURE

• Preheat oven to 350 degrees. Grease and flour two 5" x 9" loaf pans.

• Cream butter and sugar in mixer on medium speed. Add eggs and vanilla. Beat for 1-1/2 minutes.

• In a bowl, combine flour, baking soda, and salt. Add to the creamed mixture alternately with the sour cream.

• Stir in bananas and nuts. Mix until well-blended. Pour in prepared loaf pans. Bake 1 hour or until bread tests done. Serve with Tangy Cream Cheese Spread (recipe follows) for a special treat. ❏

Tangy Cream Cheese Spread

24 servings, 1 tablespoon each

INGREDIENTS

8 ounces cream cheese, softened

1/2 cup good-quality orange or other tangy fruit marmalade

PROCEDURE

• Combine cream cheese and marmalade in food processor or by hand.

• Refrigerate several hours to blend flavors. Will keep in the refrigerator a week. ❏

Date Nut Prune Bread

1 loaf (12 servings)

INGREDIENTS

1/2 cup chopped pitted dates

1/2 cup chopped pitted prunes

1 cup coarsely chopped walnuts

1-1/2 teaspoons baking soda

1/2 teaspoon salt

3 tablespoons shortening

3/4 cup boiling water

2 eggs

3/4 cup sugar

1-1/2 cups all-purpose flour

PROCEDURE

• Preheat oven to 350 degrees. Grease a 9" x 5" loaf pan.

• Combine dates, prunes, walnuts, baking soda, salt, and shortening in a bowl. Pour in the boiling water. Stir well. Let stand for 15 minutes.

• In another bowl, beat the eggs and sugar together with a fork. Add flour. Stir. (Dough will be too stiff to mix very well, but that's okay.)

• Add the date mixture. Mix until batter is well-blended. Pour into the prepared loaf pan. Bake for 1 hour or until a toothpick inserted in the center comes out clean. Serve with Tangy Cream Cheese Spread. ❏

Apple Butter Muffins

36 muffins

These muffins freeze very well. Use paper liners in the muffin tins.

INGREDIENTS

For the batter:

1/2 pound (2 sticks) unsalted butter, softened

1-1/2 cups sugar

4-1/2 cups all-purpose flour

2-1/2 tablespoons baking powder

3/4 teaspoon salt

1-1/2 teaspoons ground nutmeg

3 eggs

1-1/2 cups milk

3/4 cup apple butter

For the topping:

1/2 pound (2 sticks) butter, melted

1 tablespoon cinnamon

1-1/2 cups sugar

PROCEDURE

• Preheat oven to 350 degrees.

• In the bowl of a mixer on medium speed, cream butter and sugar until fluffy.

• In a separate bowl, sift flour, baking powder, salt, and nutmeg together.

• Combine eggs with butter and sugar in mixer bowl. Add flour mixture alternately with milk, mixing until well blended.

• Line muffin tins with paper liners. Divide batter in half. Distribute half the batter evenly among 36 muffin cups. Make a depression in the batter in each cup. Fill each depression with a generous teaspoon of apple butter. Divide remaining batter among muffin cups, spreading batter to cover apple butter.

• Bake 20 to 25 minutes, until golden brown. Let cool five minutes. Mix cinnamon and sugar for topping. Dip top of each muffin in melted butter, then in cinnamon sugar. ❑

Blintz Casserole

12 servings

This brunch dish is rich and slightly sweet. Make it up the night before and pop it in the oven early in the morning. (It takes a while to cook.) Serve with mixed fruit and good sausages or Canadian bacon.

INGREDIENTS

For the filling:

2 pounds ricotta cheese

2 eggs

1/4 cup sugar

1/8 teaspoon salt

1/4 cup fresh lemon juice

8 ounces cream cheese, softened

For the batter:

1/2 pound (2 sticks) butter, melted

2 eggs

1/2 cup sugar

1 cup sifted flour

1 tablespoon baking powder

1/8 teaspoon salt

1/4 cup milk

1 teaspoon vanilla extract

PROCEDURE

• Place ricotta cheese, eggs, sugar, salt, lemon juice, and cream cheese in mixer. Blend well. Set aside.

• Mix the remaining ingredients by hand to make the batter.

• Spoon half the batter into a greased 9" x 13" baking dish. Spread filling on top. Spread remaining batter over filling. Cover and refrigerate overnight.

• Remove casserole from refrigerator. Preheat oven to 300 degrees. Bake, uncovered, for 1-1/2 hours. ❑

Scrambled Egg Casserole

8 servings

This has been a Glen Ella Springs favorite Saturday morning breakfast for several years. The innkeepers say they love its versatility – the ingredients can be prepared ahead and assembled in the morning (which they say is what they usually do) or it can be prepared, baked ahead, refrigerated (or frozen!), and reheated just before serving. Reheating instructions are included below.

INGREDIENTS

For the vegetables:

2 tablespoons butter

1/2 cup chopped cooked ham

1/4 cup chopped green onions

1/2 cup sliced mushrooms

1/2 cup chopped Roma tomatoes

5 ounces (half a 10-ounce package) frozen chopped spinach, thawed and drained

For the cheese sauce:

2 tablespoons butter

2-1/2 tablespoons flour

2 cups milk

1/2 teaspoon salt

1/4 teaspoon pepper

1 cup shredded sharp cheddar cheese

For the eggs:

1/4 teaspoon seasoned salt

8 eggs, beaten slightly

2 tablespoons butter

For the topping:

2 cups soft breadcrumbs

2 tablespoons melted butter

Nonstick cooking spray

PROCEDURE

• Melt 2 tablespoons butter in a nonstick skillet. Saute ham, green onions, mushrooms, and tomatoes until soft. Stir in the spinach. Place ham and vegetables in a colander to drain. Wipe skillet clean.

• Melt 2 tablespoons butter in a medium saucepan. Stir in flour. Cook 2 minutes, stirring with a whisk. Add milk slowly. Bring to a boil. Cook until mixture thickens, whisking constantly. Turn down heat. Add salt, pepper, and shredded cheese. Stir until cheese has melted and sauce is smooth. Correct seasonings.

• Preheat oven to 375 degrees. Add seasoned salt to eggs. Melt 2 tablespoons butter in the nonstick skillet. Soft-scramble the eggs over low heat until about half cooked, stirring often with a wooden spoon. Add two cups of cheese sauce to eggs and combine well. Remove from heat while eggs are still very soft and runny. (They will finish cooking in the oven.)

• Spray bottom of a 2-quart casserole with nonstick cooking spray. Spoon half the scrambled eggs in the bottom of the pan. Cover with sauteed vegetables and ham. Top vegetables with the rest of the scrambled eggs.

• Mix breadcrumbs with 2 tablespoons butter. Cover top of casserole with buttered breadcrumbs. Bake in oven for 15 minutes or until eggs are set and crumbs are browned.

To prepare ahead: Bake casserole in oven until eggs are barely set (about 10 minutes). Cover and refrigerate or wrap tightly and freeze.

To reheat: Thaw in refrigerator 1 day (if frozen). Heat oven to 325 degrees. Cover casserole with aluminum foil. Heat for 20 minutes (until thoroughly warm), then remove foil, raise oven temperature to 375 degrees, and heat until crumbs are browned. ❑

Afternoon Rest & Beverages for Guests

After a busy morning of sightseeing or business meetings or time at a convention or museum exhibition, an afternoon rest plus beverages and a snack can provide a welcome change of pace for your guests. It's a good time to socialize and sip, to rest weary feet, and to touch base before evening activities begin.

Let the season and the weather dictate your choice of refreshments: hot tea or cider is wonderful on a cold day; iced tea or lemonade or sangria is cooling in the summertime. Almost everyone is happy to munch on cookies just about any time of year. Fresh fruits in season – ripe peaches or berries in summer, crisp apples in the fall – or dried fruits and nuts are healthy snacks. Here are some serving ideas:

• Summer Tea in the Garden
An old tool box or primitive wooden crate is a perfect container for transporting beverages for a casual afternoon tea. Fill it with a jar of tea, ice-filled glasses, and sliced citrus. Add cloth napkins and a picnic tablecloth and carry it to the garden to provide a refreshing break.

• A Formal Floral Tea
Invite a few friends in to meet your guest(s) and set out a formal tea like the one pictured at right. Drape the table with vintage linens and use an assortment of floral-patterned china cups, saucers, and plates for serving. Food can be simple – cookies or a tea bread, yogurt-covered raisins or other candies. (Choose foods that don't require a fork.)

• Coffee by the Fire
On a cold winter day, light a fire in the fireplace and invite guests to settle down in some easy chairs and put their feet up for a cozy coffee break. Serve cookies or pumpkin bread and use cinnamon sticks as coffee stirrers.

• A Spot of Sherry
Set out a decanter of sherry on a silver tray with an assortment of pretty glasses for sipping. Include a dish of roasted almonds and berries or other fresh fruit.

• Wine and Cheese
A bottle of wine, a thinly sliced baguette, some soft goat cheese, and a few olives in a pottery dish make a simple, hearty, Mediterranean-inspired snack. Be sure to bring out some brightly colored paper napkins.

LEMONADE BREAK

Lemons, sugar, and water – what could be more simple? Or more refreshing on a hot summer day? Ice water travels in a green glass jar. For this casual service, combine various pieces of green glass and small clear milk jugs or glasses for serving up the lemonade. Be sure to provide straws for sipping. The vintage tablecloth with yellow roses and green leaves looks wonderful with the green glass; a vintage soda-fountain jar holds the straws. Even if you make your lemonade from frozen concentrate, you could dress it up with slices of lemon or some sprigs of fresh mint.

AFTERNOON SNACKS

Handmade pottery drinking glasses are lined with squares of parchment paper and filled with dried fruits and nuts and slices of hearty bread. People can fill the glass with warm cider and munch the nibbles. Everything can be prepared ahead of time.

Gifts for Your Guests

Usually it's the guest, not the host, who presents a gift, but for a special guest or a special visit, you may wish to give more than your hospitality to commemorate the occasion. A photograph of you with your guest or a small album with photos of the visit can be put together quickly, thanks to one-hour photo developing. Or choose a souvenir that's a remembrance of where you live or a place you visited together. Gifts of food – especially something that could be enjoyed on the trip home – are other good choices. So is something you made yourself.

Rose and Angels Decoupage Plate

A plain glass plate is transformed with calligraphy and decoupage.
Designed by Ginger Hansen Shafer for Plaid Enterprises, Inc.

SUPPLIES

Clear glass plate

Decoupage finish

Decoupage paper or gift wrap printed with angels and roses

Gold spray paint

Gold acrylic craft paint

Calligraphy marker

Gold marker

White tissue paper

Clear sealer

Wax pencil

Masking tape

Sponge

Scissors

Protractor

INSTRUCTIONS

1. Cut out rose and angel prints from papers with scissors.

2. Arrange cutouts to be placed around rim of plate, using photo as a guide. Tape in place. Trace around cutouts on front of plate with a wax pencil. Remove cutouts and tape.

3. Brush decoupage medium on the **front** sides of the cutouts and glue in place on the **back** of the plate. (While you're gluing, the images will be face down, but will show through the front of the plate.)

4. Outline images with the gold marker.

5. Use the calligraphy marker to write the Bible verse on a piece of plain paper. Make a photocopy of the calligraphy. Cut out a paper circle from the photocopy with the calligraphy that is the same size as the center of the back of the plate, using the protractor to mark the circle.

6. Use a moistened sponge to tint the cutout photocopy with gold craft paint. Let dry completely.

7. Brush decoupage medium on the **front** of the paper circle. Glue to the **back** side of the plate, face down, so the verse shows from the front. Let dry.

8. Place plate on tissue paper and trace around it. Cut out a tissue paper circle slightly larger than the plate.

9. Brush decoupage finish over the entire back of the plate. Position the tissue paper over the back of the plate. Press to adhere and smooth. Allow to dry.

10. Smooth down edges of tissue paper as needed by applying decoupage finish to the paper with your finger. Let dry.

11. Spray back of plate with gold spray paint. Let dry.

12. Brush clear sealer over the back of the plate. Let dry. Rub off any traces of wax pencil with a paper towel. ❑

Flower Garden Gift Basket

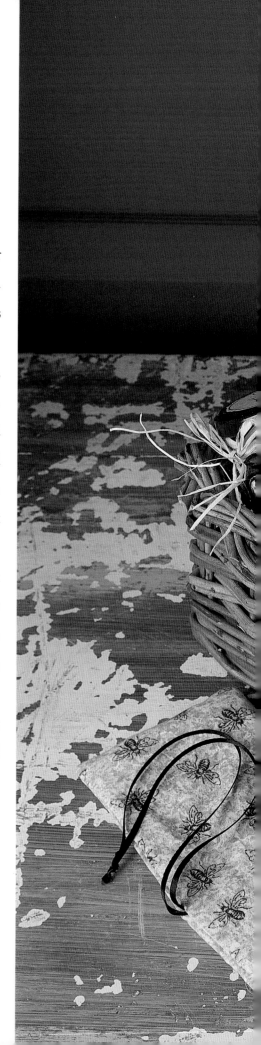

A gift basket is easy to assemble from items you make yourself or purchase and can be placed in the guest room before the guest arrives. Your guest can use some of the contents during the visit, such as foods or toiletries, and take home the rest.

Here, designer Marie Browning used the garden as her theme, choosing a bee motif to stamp labels for handmade soaps and bath oil. Other items to include in the basket might be beeswax candles, scented bath salts in envelopes decorated with photocopies of vintage seed packets, or honey-scented soaps in the shape of a bee skep. More ideas: Make bags of bee-patterned fabric to hold goodies, emboss copper plant markers to use as tags, add a bow of sheer ribbon.

With melt-and-pour soap bases and soap molds (widely available at crafts stores) and ingredients from health food and drug stores, it's easy to make your own signature soaps, bath oil, and bath salts. Be sure to label your own creations, listing ingredients and including instructions for use.

For more soap-making projects, see these books by Marie Browning: Melt & Pour Soapmaking, 300 Handcrafted Soaps, *and* Designer Soaps; *all published by Sterling Publishing, Co.*

Recipes for Flower Garden Gift Basket

RELAXING BATH SALTS

Mix in a glass bowl:

1 cup sea salt

1 cup baking soda

1 cup Epsom salts

Add:

10 drops lavender essential oil

10 drops clary sage essential oil

Mix to blend. Package in decorated envelopes or a glass jar. ❏

HONEY BEE SOAP

This soap is smooth and lightly fragranced. It is molded in a beehive candle mold.

Melt in a double boiler and hold over hot water:
1 tablespoon beeswax

Melt in a microwave oven or on top of the stove in a double boiler:
1 cup opaque melt and pour soap base

Add:
1 tablespoon honey

Mix hot melted soap and melted beeswax. Add the honey and stir until melted. Pour into prepared mold. Let harden. Unmold. Cure on a drying rack. ❏

BLACKBERRY BLISS FOAMING BATH OIL

Combine:

1/2 cup mild liquid soap

1 tablespoon glycerin

1/2 cup castor oil

1/2 cup almond oil

12 drops blackberry scenting oil

6 drops bayberry scenting oil

Mix ingredients well and pour in a bottle – they will turn nice and milky but will soon separate into three layers. Shake before use. ❏

etric Conversion Chart

Inches to Millimeters and Centimeters

Inches	mm	cm
1/8	3	.3
1/4	6	.6
3/8	10	1.0
1/2	13	1.3
5/8	16	1.6
3/4	19	1.9
7/8	22	2.2
1	25	2.5
1-1/4	32	3.2
1-1/2	38	3.8
1-3/4	44	4.4
2	51	5.1
3	76	7.6
4	102	10.2
5	127	12.7
6	152	15.2
7	178	17.8
8	203	20.3
9	229	22.9
10	254	25.4
11	279	27.9
12	305	30.5

Yards to Meters

Yards	Meters
1/8	.11
1/4	.23
3/8	.34
1/2	.46
5/8	.57
3/4	.69
7/8	.80
1	.91
2	1.83
3	2.74
4	3.66
5	4.57
6	5.49
7	6.40
8	7.32
9	8.23
10	9.14

Index